EASY UKULELE PLAY-ALONG

CLASSIC ROCK F

T0048286

Uke 'An Jam

About the TNT Changer

Use the TNT software to change keys, loop playback, and mute tracks for play-along. For complete instructions, see the *TnT ReadMe.pdf* file on your enhanced CD.

Windows users: insert the CD into your computer, double-click on My Computer, right-click on your CD drive icon, and select Explore to locate the file.

Mac users: insert the CD into your computer and double-click on the CD icon on your desktop to locate the file.

Produced by
Alfred Music Publishing Co., Inc.
P.O. Box 10003
Van Nuys, CA 91410-0003
alfred.com

Printed in USA.

Cover photo: Jacob Jeffries, © Gabby Groten.
Used by permission.
Photographer: Gabby Groten
For more on the Jacob Jeffries Band,
go to www.JacobJeffriesBand.com

Recordings: Chauncey Gardiner Combo, featuring Erick
Lynen on vocals and Armando Strange on ukulele

ISBN-10: 0-7390-7971-9 (Book & CD)
ISBN-13: 978-0-7390-7971-3 (Book & CD)

 Alfred Cares. Contents printed on 100% recycled paper.

Contents

* For minus-vocals and minus-ukulele versions, use the TNT software.

ANOTHER BRICK IN THE WALL (PART 2)

Words and Music by
ROGER WATERS

Moderately ♩ = 104

*Verse:

Dm

Uke

mf

We don't need_ no ed-u-ca-tion.

*2nd time sung by children's chorus 8va.
**Tacet first two measures on repeat.

5 Cont. simile

We don't need_ no thought con-trol._ No dark sar-cas- m

10

in the class-room. { Teach - er / Teach -ers } leave_them kids a - lone._

G

15

Elec. Gtr. 1

Another Brick in the Wall (Part 2) - 3 - 1

Another Brick in the Wall (Part 2) - 3 - 2

6

GIMME SOME LOVIN'

Words and Music by
STEVE WINWOOD, MUFF WINWOOD
and SPENCER DAVIS

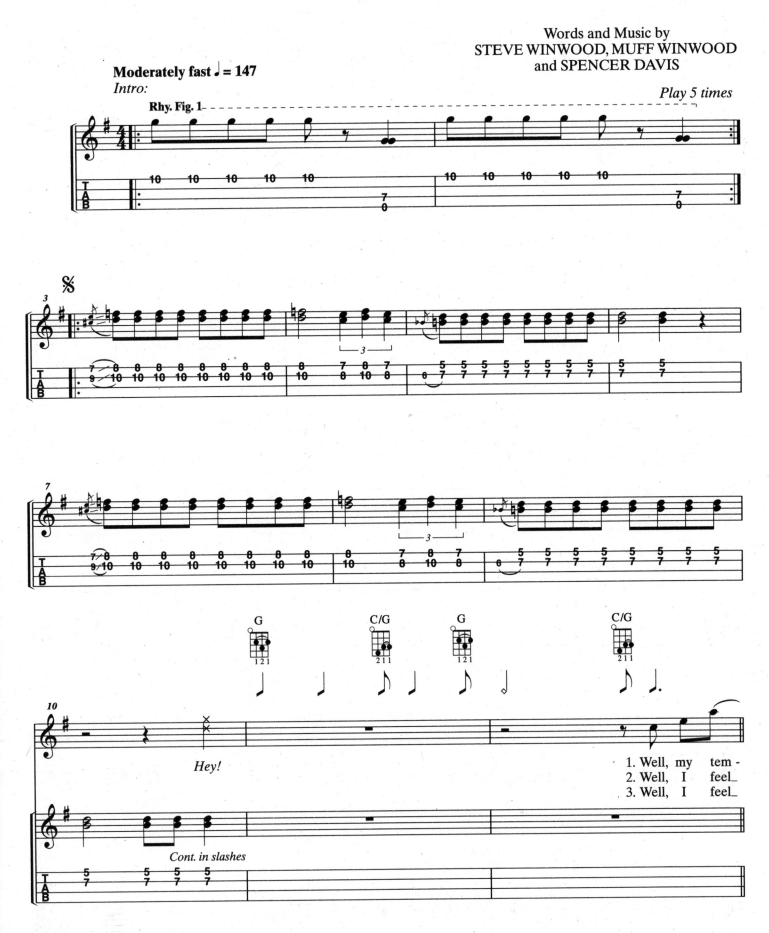

Gimme Some Lovin' - 3 - 1

*w/Lead vocal ad lib. on repeats.

BAD TO THE BONE

Open G tuning:
④ = G　②= B
③ = D　①= G

Words and Music by
GEORGE THOROGOOD

Moderately ♩ = 98

Bad to the Bone - 4 - 1

𝄉 *Verses 1, 2, & 4:*

whoo, bad to the bone.

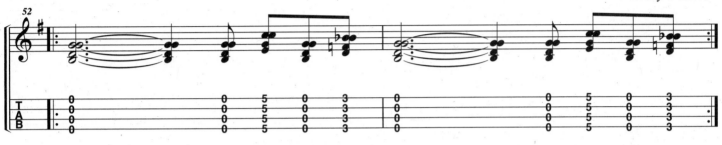

Verse 2:
I broke a thousand hearts
Before I met you.
I'll break a thousand more, baby,
Before I am through.
I wanna be yours, pretty baby,
Yours and yours alone.
I'm here to tell ya, honey,
That I'm bad to the bone,
Bad to the bone.
B-b-b-b-b-b-b bad,
B-b-b-b-b-b-b bad.
B-b-b-b-b-b-b bad,
Bad to the bone.
(To Guitar Solo 1:)

Verse 4:
Now, when I walk the streets,
Kings and Queens step aside.
Every woman I meet, heh, heh,
They all stay satisfied.
I wanna tell you, pretty baby,
What I see I make my own.
And I'm here to tell ya, honey,
That I'm bad to the bone,
Bad to the bone.
B-b-b-b-b-b-b bad,
B-b-b-b-b-b-b bad.
B-b-b-b-b-b-b bad,
Whoo, bad to the bone.
(To Outro:)

DON'T STOP BELIEVIN'

Words and Music by
JONATHAN CAIN, NEAL SCHON
and STEVE PERRY

Don't Stop Believin' - 4 - 1

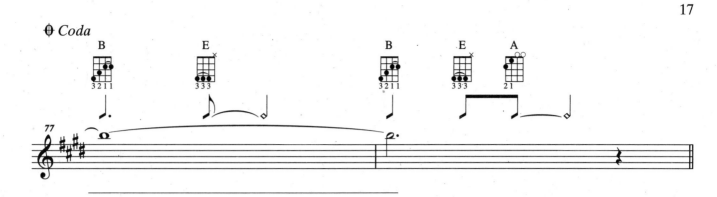

Guitar Solo:

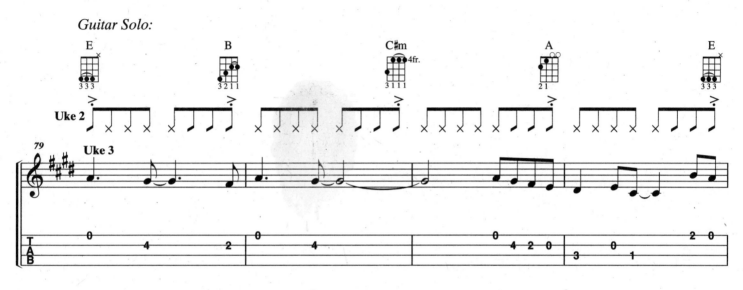

Chorus:

Don't_ stop   be - liev - in'.   Hold on to that   feel - in',_____

Repeat ad lib. and fade

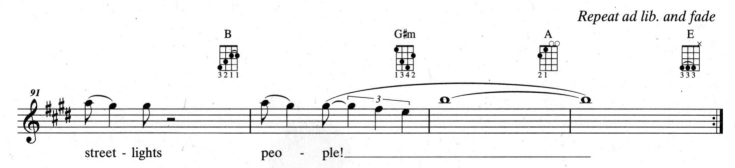

street - lights   peo — ple!_____

HOTEL CALIFORNIA

Words and Music by
DON HENLEY, GLENN FREY
and DON FELDER

Hotel California - 4 - 1

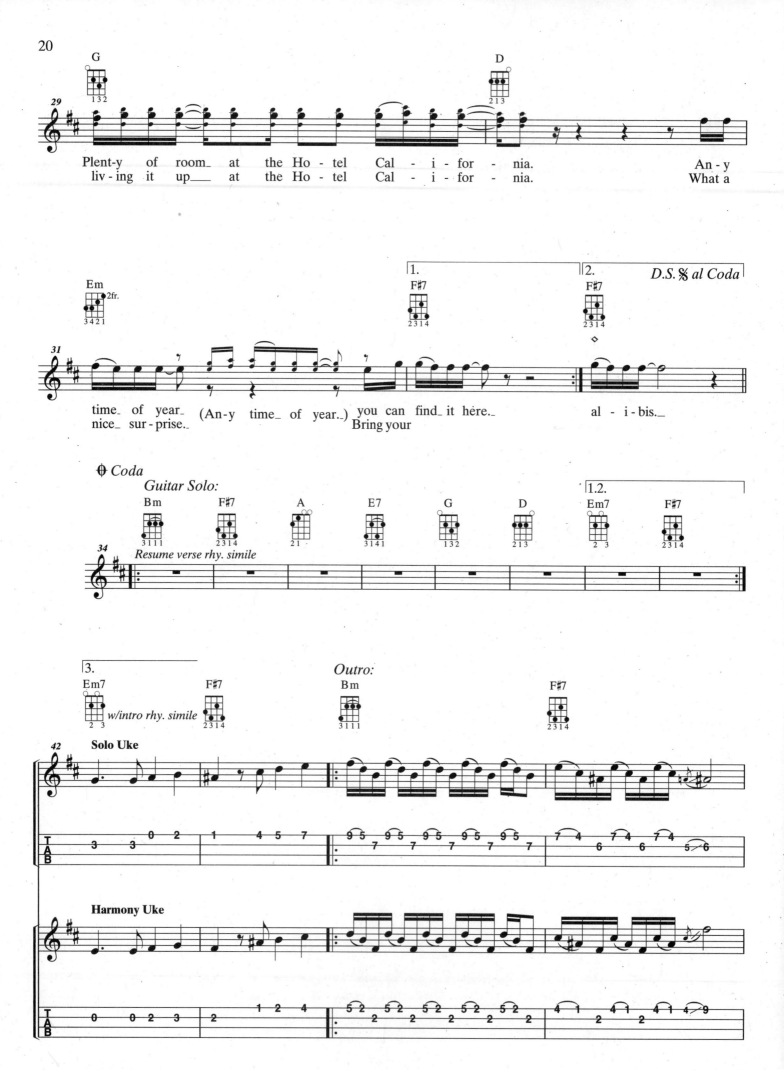

Repeat and fade

Verse 3:
Mirrors on the ceiling, the pink champagne on ice.
And she said, "We are all just prisoners here of our own device."
And in the master's chambers they gathered for the feast.
They stab it with their steely knives but they just can't kill the beast.
Last thing I remember I was running for the door.
I had to find the passage back to the place I was before.
"Relax," said the nightman, "We are programmed to receive."
You can check out anytime you like but you can never leave.

LONG TRAIN RUNNIN'

Tempo ♩ = 116

Intro:

Words and Music by
TOM JOHNSTON

Rhy. Fig. 1

Rhy. Fig. 2

1. Down a-round the cor-ner, half a mile from here, you
2.–6. *See additional lyrics*

see them old trains run-nin' and you watch them dis-ap-pear. With-out

Long Train Runnin' - 3 - 1

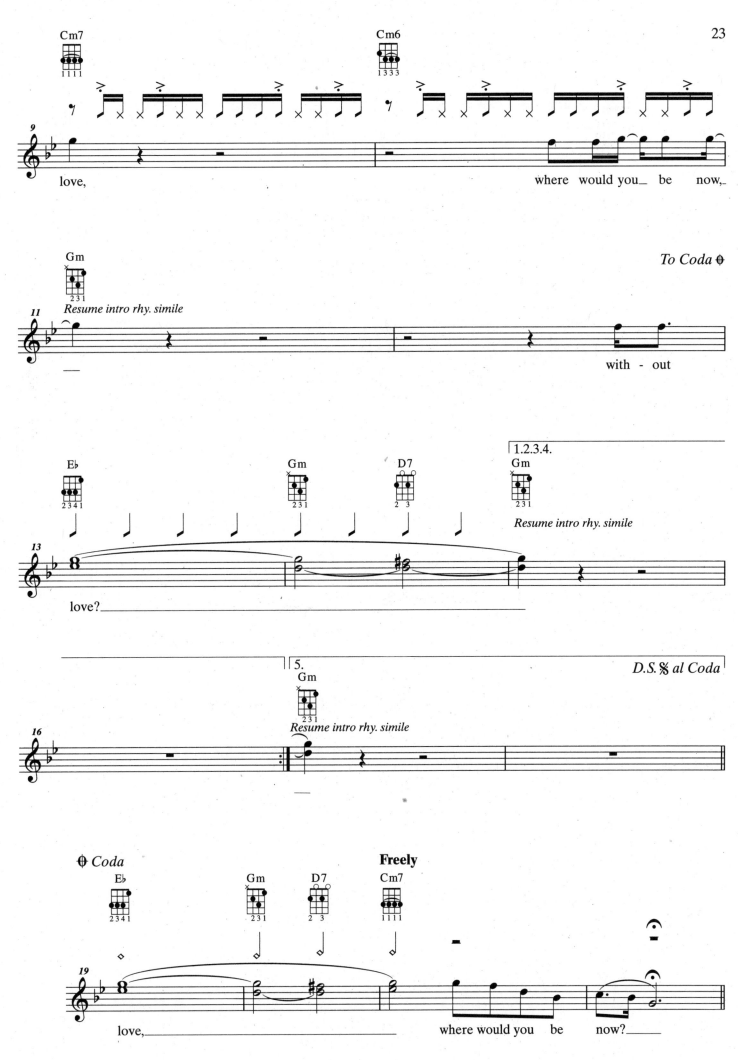

A tempo

Verse 2:
You know I saw Miss Lucy,
Down along the tracks;
She lost her home and her family,
And she won't be comin' back.
Without love, where would you be right now,
Without love?

Verses 3 & 5:
Well, the Illinois Central
And the Southern Central freight,
Gotta keep on pushin', mama,
'Cause you know they're runnin' late.
Without love, where would you be right now,
Without love?
(1st time to Verse 4:)
(2nd time to Verse 6:)

Verse 4:
Instrumental Solo
(To Verse 5:)

Verse 6:
Where pistons keep on churnin'
And the wheels go 'round and 'round,
And the steel rails are cold and hard
For the miles that they go down.
Without love, where would you be right now,
Without love?
(To Coda)

RAMBLIN' MAN

Words and Music by
FORREST RICHARD BETTS

Moderately fast ♩ = 182

Lord, I___ was born___ a ram - blin' man,_____

try'n' to make a liv - in' and do - in' the best I___ can.___ And

when it's time___ for leav - in',___ I hope you'll un - der - stand_____

that I was born___ a ram - blin' man. 1. My

Ramblin' Man - 3 - 1

SUNSHINE OF YOUR LOVE

Words and Music by
JACK BRUCE, PETE BROWN
and ERIC CLAPTON

Sunshine of Your Love - 4 - 1

STAIRWAY TO HEAVEN

Words and Music by
JIMMY PAGE and ROBERT PLANT

*With *grad. accel.* throughout song.

*With *grad. accel.* throughout song.

Stairway to Heaven - 9 - 1

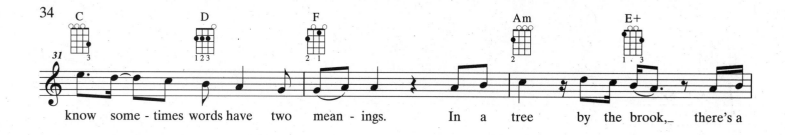

know some-times words have two mean-ings. In a tree by the brook,_ there's a

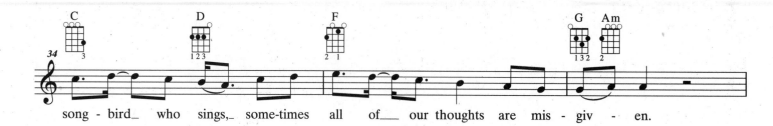

song-bird_ who sings,_ some-times all of__ our thoughts are mis-giv - en.

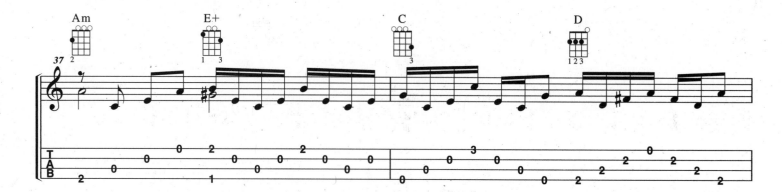

Interlude:

Rhy. Fig. 1

mf

Ooh,_____ it makes me won-

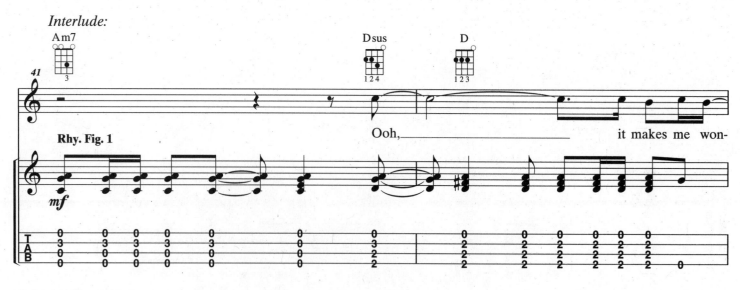

36

Interlude:

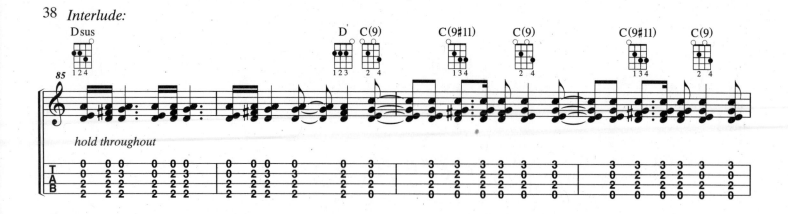

hold throughout

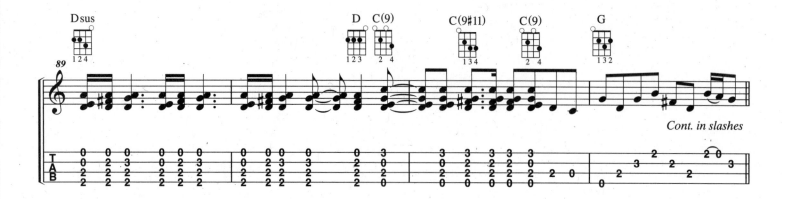

Cont. in slashes

Guitar Solo:

Play 5 times

Bridge:

And as we wind_ on down the road,___

our shad-ows tall-er than our soul._____

WILD NIGHT

Moderately fast ♩ = 148

Words and Music by
VAN MORRISON

*See TAB for riff played over the G chord throughout.

TABLATURE EXPLANATION

TAB illustrates the four strings of the ukulele.
Notes and chords are indicated by the placement of fret numbers on each string.

Standard ukulele tuning for soprano, concert, and tenor models is G–C–E–A with the fourth string tuned a whole step lower than the open 1st string.

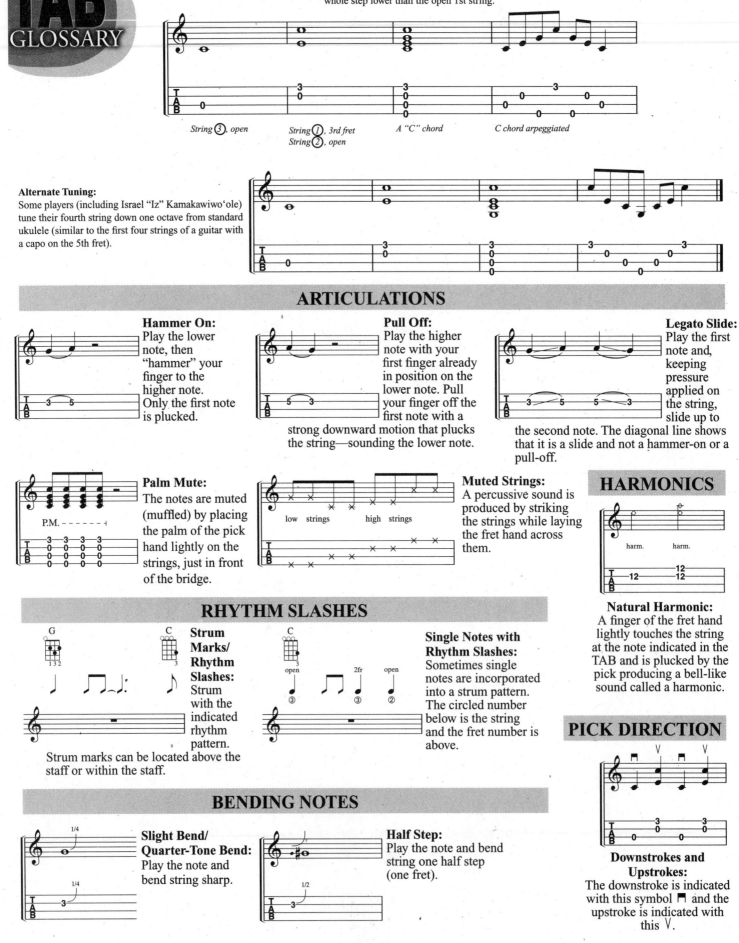

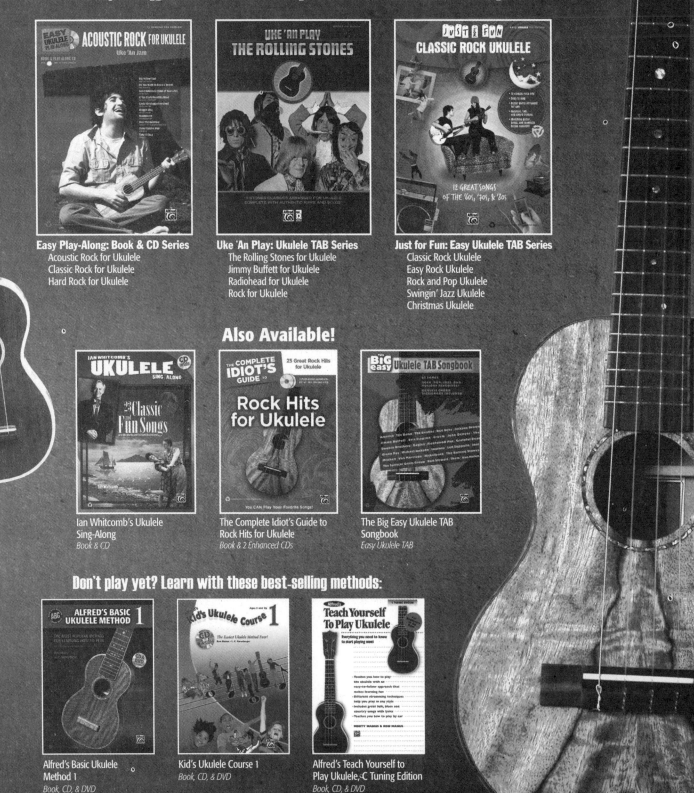